TORNADO ALERT

by Franklyn M. Branley   illustrated by Giulio Maestro

Thomas Y. Crowell   New York

LET'S READ-AND-FIND-OUT BOOK CLUB EDITION

The *Let's-Read-and-Find-Out Science Book* series was originated by Dr. Franklyn M. Branley, Astronomer Emeritus and former Chairman of the American Museum–Hayden Planetarium, and was formerly co-edited by him and Dr. Roma Gans, Professor Emeritus of Childhood Education, Teachers College, Columbia University.

Let's-Read-and-Find-Out Science Book is a registered trademark of Harper & Row, Publishers, Inc.

Library of Congress Cataloging-in-Publication Data
Branley, Franklyn Mansfield, 1915-
    Tornado alert / by Franklyn M. Branley ; illustrated by
Giulio Maestro.—1st ed.
      p.   cm.—(A Let's-read-and-find-out science book)
    Summary: Describes the origin and nature of
tornadoes and how to stay safe when threatened by one of
these dangerous storms.
    ISBN 0-690-04686-3 : $
    ISBN 0-690-04688-X (lib. bdg.) : $
    1. Tornadoes—Juvenile literature.   2. Tornadoes—
United States—Juvenile literature.   3. Storms—Juvenile
literature.   [1. Tornadoes.]   I. Maestro, Giulio, ill.
II. Title.   III. Series.
QC955.B73 1988   87-29379
551.5'53—dc19   CIP
                                                      AC

Tornadoes are powerful storms.

On a tornado day the air is hot and still.

Clouds build up rapidly. They get thick and dark.

In the distance there is thunder and lightning,

rain and hail.

Here and there parts of the clouds seem to reach toward the ground. Should these parts grow larger and become funnel shaped, watch out. The funnels could become tornadoes.

The funnel of a tornado is usually dark gray or
black. It may also be yellowish or red.

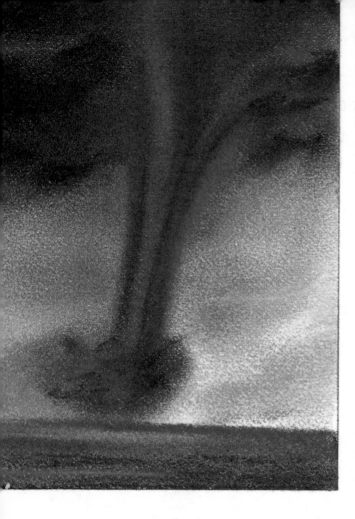

The colors come from red and yellow dirt picked
up by the tornado as it moves along the ground.

Tornadoes can strike most anywhere, but usually they happen where there is a lot of flat land. Most tornadoes occur in Texas, Oklahoma, Kansas, Nebraska, Iowa, and Missouri. Florida also has a lot of tornadoes.

Tornadoes can touch down over seas and lakes.
When that happens, they are called waterspouts.

Most tornadoes occur during April, May, and June. That's when cold air meets warm air near the Earth's surface. The cold air pushes under the warm air. The warm air is lighter than the cold air and rises rapidly.

As the warm air moves upward, it spins around, or twists. That's why tornadoes are sometimes called twisters. Some people call them cyclones. The wind speed around the funnel of the tornado may reach 300 miles an hour. No other wind on Earth blows that fast.

Cold Air

Warm Air

As the hot air rises, it also spreads out. It makes a funnel of air, with the small part of the funnel touching the ground and the large part in the dark clouds. Air all around the tornado moves in toward the funnel. At the same time, storm winds push the twisting funnel, moving it along the Earth.

During tornado season in the United States, there may be 40 or 50 tornadoes in one week. Sometimes there are many more. Most are small. Usually a tornado blows itself out in less than an hour. Some last only a few seconds.

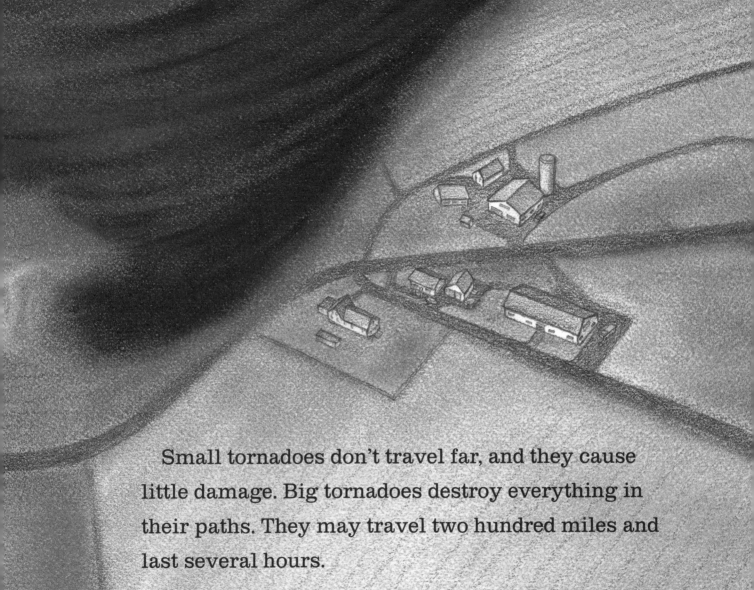

Small tornadoes don't travel far, and they cause little damage. Big tornadoes destroy everything in their paths. They may travel two hundred miles and last several hours.

During a tornado there is thunder and lightning, rain and hail. And there is lots of noise. It can sound as loud as a freight train or a jet engine. The word *tornado* comes from a Latin word that means thunder. Some of the noise does come from thunder, but most of it comes from the roaring wind. There is lots of noise, and lots and lots of wind.

Tornadoes are very powerful, and some cause a
lot of damage. Tornadoes can pick up branches and
boards, stones and bricks, cars, and sometimes even
people.

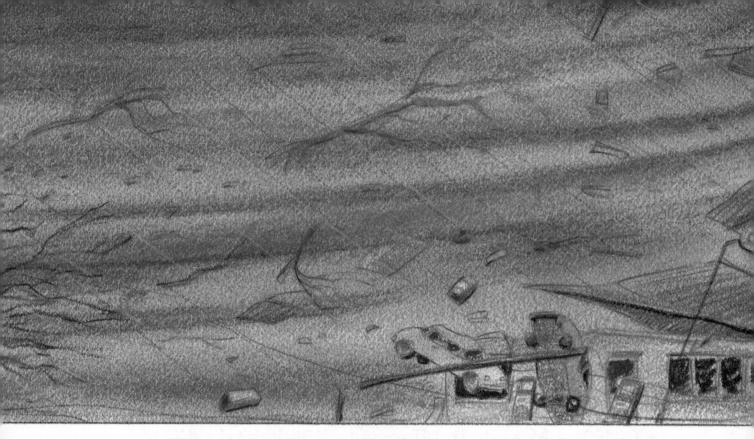

They can rip off roofs and leave a trail of wrecked houses. A tornado's path may be only 20 or 30 feet wide. Or it might be 1000 feet or more—maybe even a mile.

In 1931 a tornado in Minnesota lifted a train off its
tracks. The train and its passengers were carried
through the air and dropped 80 feet from the tracks.
There were 170 people on board. Though many

people were hurt, only one person was killed. But
in 1974 a series of tornadoes in Missouri, Illinois,
Indiana, and ten other states killed 315 people in
twenty-four hours.

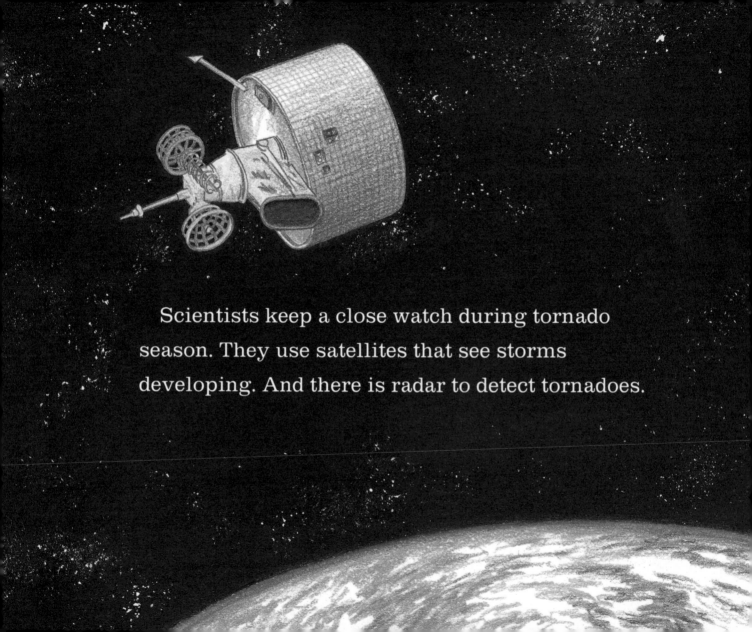

Scientists keep a close watch during tornado
season. They use satellites that see storms
developing. And there is radar to detect tornadoes.

Tornado spotters are people who watch for tornadoes. They tell radio and television stations to warn people about tornadoes while the twisters are still far away. The warnings tell people to go to a safe spot, where the tornado can't hurt them.

If a tornado is on its way, here's what you should do. Go to a nearby storm cellar. Storm cellars are underground rooms with heavy doors. They are safe.

If you are in a mobile home, get out of it. A tornado can rip apart a mobile home, even when it is tied down with strong cables. Lie face down in a ditch and cover your head with your hands. When you're in a ditch, sticks and stones flying through the air can't hit you.

If you are in a house, go to the basement and
crouch under the stairs or under a heavy workbench.
Or go to a closet that is far from an outside wall. Be
sure to keep far away from windows. The wind could
smash them and send splinters of glass through
the air.

If you are in school, follow directions. Your teacher will take you to a basement or to an inside hall. Crouch on your knees near an inner wall. Bend over and clasp your hands behind your head. Most important, keep away from glass windows.

If you are out in the country in a car, don't try to
race the tornado. Get out, and find a ditch to lie in.

When there's a tornado, there is also thunder and lightning. So keep away from metal things and from anything that uses electricity. Lightning can travel along metal pipes, and also along electric and telephone wires.

Listen to a battery radio. The radio will tell you when the storm has passed by. Stay where you are safe until you are sure the tornado is over.

Tornadoes are scary. Even if you are not right in the funnel, there is heavy rain all around, dark skies, thunder, lightning, and lots of wind. Often there will be hailstones. They may be as big as golf balls, or even bigger.

Don't panic. Know what to do when there is a
tornado. And know where to go.

There is no way to stop tornadoes. But you can be
safe from them when you know what to do.